For Izi, my family, and, my younger self...
You did it!

spring

Spring Is My Favourite Season

You appeared to me

like blossom trees in spring -

nowhere, until all at once.

Spending our nights

eating our body weights in peaches,

lighting matches

and throwing them into the lake.

Requesting you play

'Norwegian Wood' on your guitar

for the seventh time in a row.

I ask myself why, as you stroke your thumb

down my chest, and my only thought was

how you could twist my ribs in half,

and break me like an apple.

Stranger

I recalled which side of the bed you were facing

when I felt your breath

on my cold naked shoulder.

Jealousy chews at my gums,

kissing teeth and your pillow

smells of another woman's perfume.

Every Time

Since you have mentioned blossom trees

they're all I ever notice.

Now I use them as a way to count:

"Only six blossom trees until I see you."

We only get to see

blossom trees in spring

and you my love,

will soon be every day.

All I Ever See, Think, Feel, Touch or Want to Know is
You

-

Admiring the bulbs on an orchid branch,

taking it in turns

to watch each other grow.

Pisces Lover

Wake up to the sound of waves

you held me as if you were drinking from a lake

I was your only source

Fate

Loving someone is setting them free

to come back years later

to realise feelings were there along

but never revealing how much.

Time for me to be late for trains,

and for you to go back home.

Wearing the jumpers I now own.

We were kids, both blonde and foolish.

I knew then, how I would feel now.

The love we have, I will treasure forever.

My never dying flowers

agree

summer

Cherry Tree Drive

I'm in favour of the colour red.

Your sweet bite of apple,

on strawberry perfumed blankets

and a stain of red wine

on your creased white shirt.

How the flowers bloomed at the sound of your name

underneath, fire-lit skies,

laying with you in crimson fields,

right next to *Cherry Tree Drive*

where you called me your "rose" making me blush.

Couldn't see past the rosy-tinted glow,

of your so-called, passionate ways.

Stood in your Mother's dress, to soon

match my bloody nose.

I'm no longer, in favour of the colour red.

The Prince of Orange

I was only an orange to you,

a nectarine living inside

your cupboard or

placed in a bowl.

You ate me in the shower

and loved the sound

of tearing me open,

and watching the juices drip out.

Bit by bit, you dug your nails in and

forced away everything until

it was revealed to you.

Your yellow stained fingers,

managing to dig out every pip

from inside my lungs.

Puffer fish

One night while I was asleep

a puffer fish swam down my throat

and made a home inside my belly.

My mouth filled with blood

as I choked on its pointed spikes,

as the pain spread up my spine.

I remember a man watching me at the end of the bed,

dressed as a ghost in a lab-coat

with a clipboard and pen.

He told me he could remove the puffer fish,

by putting my body to sleep and

slicing my belly in two,

leaving me an empty shade of coral-

"Congratulations, it's a girl."

Morning Light

Just a little longer I insisted.

The morning light disrupted your sleep,

and you turn your head away from me.

I decided to leave you alone, admiring the

gap in your closed lips,

and tried not to make a noise, in case you

awoke,

to tell me that you no longer loved me

or recognise the person I have become.

And, if I possessed the courage to ask if you

still wanted me,

I already knew the answer.

That is why I was afraid.

That this would be the last time,

we would be laid together in this bed.

We fell apart,

still wearing your favourite jumper.

autumn

Final Moments before Sleep

I place my glasses on the side
watching you turn from perfectly clear
then as if your body left a shape in our room.

You would leave the water on,
remains of you left on the shower walls-
a masterpiece made from honey locks.

A memory of your silhouette
standing in the lit doorway
I wish I took a photograph
because then I could see you again.

Brushing your teeth

while only wearing my underwear.

A pool of peppermint and blood

still stained in the bathroom sink.

You lit a candle and left the match on the side,

you appeared on the ceiling

dancing with the flickering candle flame.

We let it burn,

overnight.

Your Perspective

Have you noticed

there's a tree in your garden

that's in the shape of a dragon?

Sometimes, I see it in my dreams

and think of it

when you stroke my knuckles

counter clockwise

or when my nose starts to bleed

on the train to see you.

Oh, to be that dragon,

getting to watch over you

as you sleep

or when you stand in the window

drinking your morning burnt coffee.

Oblivious to the world,

not realising a dragon is there,

looking after you.

Library

Your body was a library,

 that I wanted to inspect every shelf

and get familiar with,

until I found my favourite spot.

Once, you told me

"I can read you like a book"

when your shelves were empty all long,

your lies were only metaphors

and you had no intention

of even turning a page

or reading a single sentence.

Fathers

Men are not being taught

The meaning of consent

Boys are being taught

if you pull someone's hair

it means they love you-

but it doesn't feel that way

when they have your head forced into their pillow.

Fathers believe it is a crime for their teenager

wearing lipstick

When the crime has been them all along

Because they're not just old men at bus stops
They stare at you in the bath

In the cracks of the door

And know how to say hateful things

Fathers really do know how to say hurtful things

Cobweb Man

There is a cobweb in the attic

that reminds me of a man

who used to know me.

It covers the possessions of unopened boxes

with photographs of a man

with hair black as ink,

holding a child.

The deep lines on his forehead

that make out out the pattern

of a cobweb.

Here is the woman

that knows the man

who used to know me.

Her sickly smell of peppermint

and stains down her blue uniform.

She reassures me, he's getting better.

I come back every Saturday

but he doesn't say a word to me-

"Hello Dad, how are you?"

He is still the man who used to know me.

Enjoy

We have sex like actors

I pretend to enjoy it

I still let you finish

winter

Augustus

Our love became less familiar,

lilies in a vase that needed to be replaced.

Our love wouldn't last another glorious Summer.

August's golden flakes and fireflies waltzing,

all lie at the bottom of a swimming pool.

Our love became less familiar,

Delaying our walk home to watch the snow fall,

victim to December's rouge, the snow the colour

of a perfect smile.

Our love became less familiar,

Memories now fall like hail,

to summon the thought of us together.

Only a trail of gold left behind.

Now that you.re not here, is now familiar.

Christmas Morning

The door handle breaking,

shouting at midnight then driving away

All while pretending to be fast asleep.

Waking up to her empty wardrobe,

watching her remaining things being thrown

away.

A cracked photograph remains closed inside

a dresser drawer.

But the dust prints remain.

I don't think I'll ever get used to seeing my

Mother,

without her wedding ring on.

Thank you to Izak, for everything for bringing my spark back.

Thank you to Mary for being my most longest and cherished friendship, I am so proud of you every single day.

To my Dad, who is my absolute hero and the funniest man I've ever met (he told me to say this) I love you so much.

To my Grandma, who probably shouldn't read this

To my sister, you have been nothing but the greatest role model to me.

I hope to make all of my friends and family proud and my future self, hey you've done it! You've finally got a book on your shelves with your name on.